Recipes by Neelam Pokhrel
Design by Nabin Niroula

www.veganbell.com

Thank you for entrusting your time and money on our Vegan In An Instant Cookbook. We have covered our absolute favorite pressure cooker recipes in here.

Like you, we hate purchasing a cookbook that asks for a weird list of ingredients that aren't readily available. So considerable attention has been given to make sure the ingredients are easily accessible in your local grocery or online.

You might wonder why there isn't a beginner's 'manual' to operate your electric pressure cooker. It is because our instructions/directions are super detailed and simple to grasp and follow.

If you've just purchased your first electric pressure cooker (Instant Pot), you're in good hands.

Grains

Minty Farro Salad   6

Kamut Salad with Arugula   8

Veggie Quiona Salad   9

Ginger Barley Salad   10

Eggplant Freekeh   12

Biryani Rice   13

Mexican Quinoa   15

Dalia Pulao   16

Herbed Polenta   18

Buckwheat Risotto with Mushroom   19

3 Minutes Instant Oats   20

Pumpkin-Spice Oats   22

Rainbow Rice Salad   23

Kheer   24

Beans & Lentils

Baked (but not baked) beans   26

Refried Beans   27

Ethiopian Lentil Stew   28

Lentil Bolognese   30

Broccoli & Chickpea Mix   31

Mixed Beans Kwati   32

Minty Green Lentil   34

Spinach Lentil Mix   36

Dal Makhani   38

Vegan Chili   41

Veggies

Sweet and Spicy Carrots   42

Simple Artichokes with Cashew Dips 43

Cauliflower Rice   44

Asparagus Mushrooms   46

Easy Garlic Mashed Potatoes   47

Southern Delight   48

Spicy Kale   50

Steamed Garlic Soybeans   51

Mashed Broccoli   52

Zucchini Herb Summer Veggies   53

Jeera Aloo   54

The Green Bowl   56

Instant Broccoli Mushroom   57

Sesame & Napa Cabbage   58

Rosemary Potatoes   59

Aloo Gobi   60

Soups & Stews

Easy Tomato Soup   62

French Onion Cream Soup   64

Butternut Squash and Sage Soup 65

Chickpea Spinach Stew   66

Kale & Sweet Potato Soup   68

Barley Mushroom Hearty Soup   69

Kidney Beans Stew   70

Split Peas Soup   72

Black Beans Soup   73

Creamy Minty Pea Soup   74

Let's cook!

Minty Farro Salad

Mint and lemon really complement the chilies' heat in this recipe.
If you don't like it hot, simply seed the chilies before dressing.

Preparation Time: 5 minutes

Pressure Time: 15 minutes

Pressure Level: High

Pressure Vent Release: Natural

Servings: 4

Ingredients

Farro

- 1 teaspoon olive oil
- 4 garlic cloves, chopped
- 1 cup farro (whole grain), washed and drained
- 2 cups vegetable stock (or water)
- 1 bay leaf

Dressing & Toppings

- 4 garlic cloves
- ½ cup fresh mint
- ¼ cup fresh cilantro
- 1 jalapeño
- 1 hot chili (cayenne / serrano)
- 2 stalks green onion, chopped
- ½ tablespoon lemon zest
- 2 tablespoons lemon juice
- ½ teaspoon salt
- ¼ teaspoon pepper
- 2 tablespoons water
- 7 oz. (200 gm.) cherry tomatoes, halved
- ¼ cup steamed corn

Instructions

To prepare farro,

1. Press SAUTE to heat your electric pressure cooker. Once it's hot, add oil + chopped garlic and sauté for 30 seconds or until the garlics turn golden.
2. Add the farro + vegetable stock (or water) + bay leaf.
3. Secure the lid and turn the pressure knob to SEALING.
4. Press MANUAL (or "PRESSURE COOK" in newer models) and set the timer to 15 MINUTES on HIGH PRESSURE.
5. When the timer beeps, press CANCEL and let the pressure release naturally for 10 minutes. Then turn the pressure knob to VENTING and manually release any remaining pressure.
6. Remove the lid, discard the bay leaf + excessive liquid (if any), and transfer the cooked farro to a serving bowl(s).

To prepare dressing,

1. Add the garlic, fresh mint, cilantro leaves, chilies, green onions, lemon juice + zest, salt, pepper and 2 tablespoons water in a blender and blend until smooth.
2. Pour this dressing over cooked farro and mix well using forks. Add the halved cherry tomatoes, steamed corn, and diced avocado (optional) on top and serve.

Nutrition Facts (per Serving)

Calories 296 | Fat 10.6 g | Carb 57.9 g | Protein 9 g
Fiber 10.6 g

Kamut Salad with Arugula

This recipe works well with any other hearty grains like rye, wheat berries, spelt, or even whole oat groats.

Preparation Time: 5 minutes

Pressure Time: 13 minutes

Pressure Level: High

Pressure Vent Release: Natural

Servings: 2

Ingredients

- 1 teaspoon olive oil
- 1 large onion, chopped
- 4 garlic cloves, chopped
- ¼ cup sun-dried tomatoes, finely chopped
- 1 cup kamut, washed and drained
- 2 cups vegetable stock (or water)
- 1.5 tablespoons balsamic vinegar
- 2 tablespoons freshly chopped parsley
- ½ cup chopped tomatoes
- ¾ cup arugula
- Salt and freshly ground black pepper

Instructions

1. Press SAUTE to heat your electric pressure cooker. Add olive oil. Once it's hot, add half of the chopped onion and half of the chopped garlic. Stir and saute for 40-60 seconds or the onions turn golden.
2. Add chopped sun-dried tomatoes, kamut, vegetable stock (or water), salt and pepper. Give it a quick stir.
3. Secure the lid and turn the pressure knob to SEALING.
4. Press MANUAL (or "PRESSURE COOK" in newer models) and set the timer to 13 MINUTES on HIGH PRESSURE.
5. When the timer beeps, press CANCEL and allow the pressure to release naturally for 8-10 minutes. Then turn the pressure knob to VENTING and manually release the remaining pressure.
6. Remove the lid and transfer the cooked kamut to a serving bowl(s).
7. Add the remaining minced garlic + onion + vinegar + chopped parsley + tomatoes on top and toss. Serve with arugula.

Nutrition Facts (per Serving)

Calories 293 | Fat 3.4 g | Carb 60.6 g | Protein 10.7 g
Fiber 11.1 g

Veggie Quinoa Salad

Tomatillo brings a whole new level of deliciousness to this recipe with its tarty flavor and crunchy texture.

Preparation Time: 5 minutes

Pressure Time: 5 minutes

Pressure Level: High

Pressure Vent Release: Natural

Servings: 2

Ingredients

- 8 oz. / 225 gm. tomatillos (aka Mexican husk tomatoes) - husks removed and rinsed
- 4 garlic cloves, minced
- 2 tablespoons lime juice
- ¾ cup quinoa, rinsed and drained
- 1 green bell pepper - cored, deseeded, and diced
- 1 cup water (or veggie stock)
- ½ cup chopped green onions
- 3 tablespoons chopped coriander
- 1 medium tomato, diced
- Salt and pepper

Instructions

1. Chop around 4 oz. (110 gm.) tomatillos into smaller pieces and set aside.
2. In a blender, blend the remaining tomatillos + garlic + lime juice + salt + pepper until smooth. Set aside.
3. Press SAUTE to heat your electric pressure cooker.
4. Once it's hot, add the quinoa and dry-sauté for about 3 minutes (stir continuously). Add water (or veggie stock, if using).
5. Secure the lid and turn the pressure knob to SEALING.
6. Press MANUAL (or "PRESSURE COOK" in newer models) and set the timer to 5 minutes on HIGH PRESSURE.
7. Once the timer beeps, press CANCEL and allow the pressure to release naturally for 8-10 minutes. Then turn the pressure knob to VENTING and release any remaining pressure.
8. Transfer the cooked quinoa to a serving bowl. Add the tomatillo pieces, chopped green onions, coriander, diced tomato, diced bell pepper and the blended tomatillo mixture on top. Mix well and serve.

Nutrition Facts (per Serving)

Calories 329 | Fat 5.7 g | Carb 59.8 g | Protein 12.5 g
Fiber 9.4 g

Ginger Barley Salad

Despite the long list of ingredients, this gingery recipe is really easy to make. Really filling too!

Preparation Time: 5 minutes

Pressure Time: 1 minute + 13 minutes

Pressure Level: High + High

Pressure Release: Quick +Natural

Servings: 2-3

Ingredients

- ¾ cup green beans, cut into 1-inch (2.5 cm.) pieces
- 1 cup broccoli florets, sliced
- ¼ cup water
- 1.5 cups vegetable stock (or water)
- 1 cup whole (or hulled) barley, washed and drained
- 1.5 tablespoons tamari (or soy sauce)
- ½ tablespoon balsamic vinegar
- 1 teaspoon toasted sesame oil
- ½ tablespoon grated ginger
- 2 garlic cloves, minced
- ½ cup finely diced carrots
- ½ cup cucumber, diced
- ½ cup chopped green onions
- 1 tablespoon sesame seeds, toasted
- Salt and pepper

Instructions

1. Add ¼ cup water to your electric pressure cooker and place a steamer basket inside. Transfer the green beans + sliced broccoli to the basket.
2. Secure the lid and turn the pressure knob to SEALING.
3. Press MANUAL (or "PRESSURE COOK" in newer models) and set the timer to 1 MINUTE on HIGH PRESSURE.
4. When the timer beeps, press CANCEL and turn the pressure knob to VENTING. Open the lid, remove the basket, and transfer the veggies to a bowl. Set aside.
5. Drain the liquid from the cooker and add the barley + vegetable stock (or water). Secure the lid and turn the pressure knob to SEALING.
6. Press MANUAL and set the timer to 13 MINUTES on HIGH PRESSURE.
7. In the meantime, add the soy (or tamari) sauce, vinegar, sesame oil, minced garlic, grated ginger, salt and pepper to a medium mixing bowl. Mix well and set aside.
8. When the timer beeps, press CANCEL and allow the pressure to release naturally for 8-10 minutes. Then turn the pressure knob to VENTING and release the remaining pressure.
9. Open the lid and transfer the cooked barley + cooked beans + broccoli to a serving dish.
10. Add carrot, cucumber, green onions and the dressing. Stir well to combine and serve.

Nutrition Facts (per Serving)

Calories 309 | Fat 4.4 g | Carb 60.8 g | Protein 9.5 g
Fiber 11.6 g

Eggplant Freekeh

Freekeh has a smoky aroma and is comparable to bulgur. It is extremely versatile and goes along with any vegetable. TIP: You can easily replace Freekeh with Quinoa.

Preparation Time: 5 minutes

Pressure Time: 6 minutes

Pressure Level: High

Pressure Vent Release: Natural

Servings: 2

Ingredients

- ½ tablespoon olive oil
- 1 medium red onion, chopped
- 4 garlic cloves, minced
- 1 medium capsicum, chopped
- ¾ cup cracked freekeh (or quinoa)
- 1 medium-large eggplant, diced
- 1 cup veggie stock (or water)
- Salt and pepper, to taste
- 3 tablespoons freshly chopped parsley

Instructions

1. Press SAUTE to heat your electric pressure cooker. Add olive oil.
2. Once it's hot, add the chopped onion and saute for 1 minute or until translucent. Add minced garlic, chopped capsicum and cook for another minute.
3. Next add the freekeh (or quinoa), diced eggplant, vegetable stock, salt and pepper.
4. Secure the lid and turn the pressure knob to SEALING.
5. Press MANUAL (or "PRESSURE COOK" in newer models) and set the timer to 6 MINUTES on HIGH PRESSURE.
6. Once the timer beeps, press CANCEL and allow the pressure to release naturally for 8-10 minutes. Then turn the pressure knob to VENTING and release any remaining pressure.
7. Open the lid and transfer the cooked freekeh to a serving bowl. Adjust seasonings and garnish with chopped parsley.

Nutrition Facts (per Serving)

Calories 363 | Fat 8.2 g | Carb 62.3 g | Protein 12.8 g
Fiber 11.9 g

Biryani Rice

Indian-inspired rice with lots of veggies and spices.

Preparation Time: 10 minutes
Pressure Time: 2 minutes + 13 minutes
Pressure Level: High + High
Pressure Release: Quick + Natural
Servings: 2

Ingredients

- ½ cup diced carrot
- ½ cup sliced green beans
- ½ cup diced sweet potatoes (skin peeled)
- ¾ cup cauliflower florets
- ¼ cup water
- 2 tablespoons lemon juice
- 2 garlic cloves, minced
- 1 small jalapeno, minced
- 1 teaspoon grated ginger
- 1 cup vegetable stock (or water)
- 1 tablespoon olive oil
- 1 teaspoon cumin seeds
- 1 medium onion, sliced
- 1 medium tomato, chopped
- 1/2 teaspoon cumin powder
- ¾ teaspoon garam masala powder
- ¼ teaspoon turmeric powder
- 1 bay leaf
- 2 tablespoons chopped cilantro
- ¾ cup basmati rice, soaked for 40 minutes and drained
- Salt

Instructions

1. In a mixing bowl, add the diced carrots, beans, sweet potatoes, and cauliflower florets.
2. In another bowl, add lemon juice, garlic, jalapeno and ginger. Mix well and pour over the vegetables.
3. Toss and marinade for 8-10 minutes.
4. Add ¼ cup water to your electric pressure cooker and place a steamer basket inside. Transfer the marinated veggies to the basket.
5. Secure the lid and turn the pressure knob to SEALING.
6. Press MANUAL and set the timer to 2 MINUTES on HIGH PRESSURE.
7. Once the timer beeps, press CANCEL. Carefully turn the pressure knob to VENTING and release the pressure.
8. Open the lid and transfer the veggies to a bowl. Set aside.

9. Drain the cooker and press SAUTE. Add the olive oil. Once it's hot, add cumin seeds and let it splutter. Then add onions and saute until translucent.

10. Time to spice things up. Add tomatoes, cumin powder, garam masala powder, turmeric powder, and bay leaf. Stir and saute for 1 minute.

11. Next add basmati rice, 1 cup vegetable stock, and salt. Stir well.

12. Secure the lid and turn the pressure knob to SEALING. Press MANUAL (or "PRESSURE COOK" in newer models) and set the timer to 13 MINUTES on HIGH PRESSURE.

13. Once the timer beeps, press CANCEL and allow the pressure to release naturally for 8-10 minutes. Then turn the pressure knob to VENTING and release any remaining pressure.

14. Open the lid and add the marinated vegetables. Give it a gentle stir. Cover the lid and let it sit for 4-5 minutes.

15. Adjust the seasoning, garnish with chopped cilantro and serve.

Nutrition Facts (per Serving)

Calories 345 | Fat 4.2 g | Carb 70.4 g | Protein 7.7 g
Fiber 7 g

Mexican Quinoa

Preparation Time: 5 minutes

Pressure Time: 5 minutes

Pressure Level: High

Pressure Vent Release: Natural

Servings: 2-3

Ingredients

- 1 tablespoon olive oil
- 1 small red onion, chopped
- 4 garlic cloves, chopped
- 1 jalapeno, chopped
- 4 medium fire-roasted tomatoes, roughly chopped
- 1 cup frozen corn, thawed
- 2 cups black beans, cooked (15 oz. / 425 gm. canned)
- ½ teaspoon cumin powder
- ½ teaspoon smoked paprika
- ¼ teaspoon cayenne pepper
- Salt and pepper, to taste
- 1 cup quinoa, washed and drained
- 1.5 cups veggie stock (or water)
- Handful of freshly chopped cilantro
- 1 tablespoon lime juice

Instructions

1. Press SAUTE to heat your electric pressure cooker. Add olive oil.
2. Once it's hot, add onion, garlic and jalapeno. Stir and saute for 2 minutes or until the onions soften.
3. Add the tomatoes + corn + black beans and mix well.
4. Add the spices - cumin, smoked paprika, cayenne, salt, and pepper. Stir and cook for 1 minute.
5. Next stir in the quinoa. Add veggie stock (or water) and mix.
6. Secure the lid and turn the pressure knob to SEALING.
7. Press MANUAL (or "PRESSURE COOK" on newer models) and set the timer to 5 MINUTES on HIGH PRESSURE.
8. When the timer beeps, press CANCEL and allow the pressure to release naturally for 8-10 minutes. Then turn the pressure valve to VENTING and release the remaining pressure.
9. Open the lid and fluff the quinoa using a fork.
10. Transfer to a serving bowl(s). Garnish with freshly chopped cilantro and drizzle lime juice on top. Serve with avocado (optional).

Nutrition Facts (per Serving)

Calories 345 | Fat 4.2 g | Carb 70.4 g | Protein 7 g
Fiber 7 g

Dalia Pulao

Dalia (wheat porridge) is prepared using cracked wheat / barley and is an excellent morning breakfast recipe.

Preparation Time: 5 minutes

Pressure Time: 3 minutes

Pressure Level: High

Pressure Vent Release: Natural

Servings: 2

Ingredients

- 1 tablespoon coconut oil
- ½ cup dalia (cracked wheat / cracked barley / bulgur)
- ½ cup peas (fresh or frozen)
- ½ cup chopped green beans
- ½ cup chopped carrots
- Salt
- 2 cups water

Instructions

1. Select SAUTE to heat your electric pressure cooker. Add coconut oil.
2. Once it's hot, add dalia. Stir and saute for 4-5 minutes or until it turns light brown (stir continuously).
3. Add the peas, beans, and carrots. Stir and cook for 1 minute.
4. Add salt + water and give it a quick stir.
5. Secure the lid and turn the pressure knob to SEALING.
6. Press MANUAL (or "PRESSURE COOK" in newer models) and set the timer to 3 MINUTES on HIGH PRESSURE.
7. Once the timer beeps, press CANCEL and allow the pressure to release naturally for 8-10 minutes. Then turn the pressure knob to VENTING and release the remaining pressure.
8. Open the lid, transfer the pulao to a serving bowl(s) and serve.

Nutrition Facts (per Serving)

Calories 269 | Fat 6 g | Carb 47.8 g | Protein 12 g
Fiber 9.3 g

Herbed Polenta

I recommend you use coarse polenta instead of cornmeal / corn flour for this recipe.

Preparation Time: 5 minutes

Pressure Time: 10 minutes

Pressure Level: High

Pressure Vent Release: Natural

Servings: 2

Ingredients

- ½ tablespoon coconut oil
- 1 onion, finely chopped
- 4-5 garlic cloves, minced
- 2 cups veggie stock (or water)
- ½ teaspoon salt
- 1 bay leaf
- 1 teaspoon chopped oregano leaves
- 1 teaspoon chopped rosemary leaves
- 2 tablespoons chopped basil leaves
- 2 tablespoons chopped parsley
- ½ cup coarse polenta

Instructions

1. Press SAUTE to heat your electric pressure cooker. Add oil. Once it's hot, add the chopped onion and saute for 1 minute or until golden. Add minced garlic and saute for another minute.
2. Add veggie stock (or water), salt, bay leaf, chopped oregano and rosemary leaves. Give it a nice stir.
3. Add polenta on top. Do not stir.
4. Gently secure the lid and turn the pressure knob to SEALING.
5. Press MANUAL (or "PRESSURE COOK" in newer models) and set the timer to 10 MINUTES on HIGH PRESSURE.
6. Once the timer beeps, press CANCEL and allow the pressure to release naturally for 8-10 minutes. Then turn the pressure knob to VENTING release the pressure valve.
7. Open the lid and discard the bay leaf. Whisk well to smoothen any lumps. Garnish with chopped basil and parsley. Serve.

Nutrition Facts (per Serving)

Calories 203 | Fat 8.1 g | Carb 30.5 g | Protein 3.8 g
Fiber 3.7 g

Buckwheat Risotto with Mushroom

Delicious buckwheat risotto under 5 minutes.

Preparation Time: 2 minutes

Pressure Time: 3 minutes

Pressure Level: High

Pressure Vent Release: Natural

Servings: 2

Ingredients

- ½ tablespoon olive oil
- 1 onion, finely chopped
- 5 garlic cloves, minced
- ¾ cup buckwheat groats
- 1 bay leaf
- 1 cup common mushrooms, sliced
- 2 cups vegetable stock
- 2 stalks green onions, chopped
- 2 tablespoons chopped parsley
- 1 teaspoon balsamic vinegar
- Salt

Instructions

1. Press SAUTE to heat your electric pressure cooker. Add oil.
2. Once it's hot, add the chopped onion and saute for 2 minutes or until golden.
3. Add minced garlic and saute for another minute.
4. Mix in the buckwheat groats.
5. Toss in the bay leaf, and sliced mushrooms. Cook for 2 minutes (stirring frequently) then add the veggie stock.
6. Secure the lid and turn the pressure knob to SEALING.
7. Press MANUAL (or "PRESSURE COOK" in newer models) and set the timer to 3 MINUTES on HIGH PRESSURE.
8. Once the timer beeps, press CANCEL and allow the pressure to release naturally for 8-10 minutes. Then turn the pressure knob to VENTING and release the remaining pressure.
9. Gently open the lid and discard the bay leaf. Stir in chopped green onions and vinegar.
10. Season with salt, and garnish with freshly chopped parsley. Serve.

Nutrition Facts (per Serving)

Calories 295 | Fat 5.4 g | Carb 57 g | Protein 10 g
Fiber 8.5 g

3 Minutes Instant Oats

The steel-cut oats are ready within few minutes in your electric pressure cooker. You can keep them in the fridge for later use.

Preparation Time: 2 minutes

Pressure Time: 6 minutes

Pressure Level: High

Pressure Vent Release: Natural

Servings: 2

Ingredients

- 1 cup water
- 2 cups almond milk (or any dairy-free milk)
- ½ teaspoon powdered cinnamon
- 2 large apples, deseeded & chopped
- Pinch of salt
- 1 tablespoon brown sugar (optional)
- 1 cup steel-cut oats

Instructions

1. Add water, almond milk, cinnamon, apples, sugar, salt, and oats in your electric pressure cooker. Stir well.
2. Secure the lid and turn the pressure knob to SEALING.
3. Press MANUAL (or "PRESSURE COOK" in newer models) and set the timer to 6 MINUTES on HIGH PRESSURE.
4. Once the timer beeps, press CANCEL and allow the pressure to release naturally for 8-10 minutes. Then turn the pressure knob to VENTING and release the remaining pressure.
5. Gently remove the lid and give it a quick stir. Serve hot or chilled with your fav fruits and nuts.

Nutrition Facts (per Serving)

Calories 273 | Fat 3.1 g | Carb 50.7 g | Protein 6.9 g
Fiber 7 g

Pumpkin-Spice Oats

Preparation Time: 2 minutes

Pressure Time: 6 minutes

Pressure Level: High

Pressure Vent Release: Natural

Servings: 2

Ingredients

- 1 cup water
- 1 cup coconut milk (or your fav non-dairy milk)
- 1 teaspoon vanilla essence
- Pinch of salt
- Pinch of ground nutmeg
- ¼ teaspoon ground cardamom
- ½ teaspoon powdered cinnamon
- ¼ cup dried cranberries
- 2/3 cup steel-cut oats
- ½ cup pumpkin puree
- 1 teaspoon pumpkin pie spice
- 4 tablespoons toasted and chopped pecans/walnuts
- ¼ cup maple syrup

Instructions

1. Add water, coconut milk, vanilla essence, salt, nutmeg, cardamom, cinnamon, and cranberries in your electric pressure cooker. Give it a good stir.
2. Add pumpkin puree and steel-cut oats and mix well.
3. Secure the lid and turn the pressure knob to SEALING.
4. Press MANUAL (or "PRESSURE COOK" in newer models) and set the timer to 6 MINUTES on HIGH PRESSURE.
5. Once the timer beeps, press CANCEL and allow the pressure to release naturally for 8-10 minutes. Then turn the pressure knob to VENTING and release the remaining pressure.
6. Remove the lid and stir well.
7. Stir in the pumpkin spice and maple syrup. Transfer to a serving bowl. Top with toasted nuts and serve.

Nutrition Facts (per Serving)

Calories 799 | Fat 54.4 g | Carb 73.3 g | Protein 6.8 g
Fiber 5.1 g

Rainbow Rice Salad

This recipe has a lot of sweet veggies as they pair well with black rice.

Preparation Time: 5 minutes

Pressure Time: 2 minutes + 15 minutes

Pressure Level: High + High

Pressure Release: Quick + Natural

Servings: 2

Ingredients

- 1 small sweet potato, peeled and diced
- 1 small parsnip, diced
- 1 small carrot, diced
- ¼ cup water
- 1 cup black rice, rinsed
- 1 ¾ cup water
- 1 sprig shallot, minced
- 2 tablespoons freshly chopped cilantro
- 1 teaspoon grated lime zest
- 1 tablespoon lime juice
- ½ tablespoon red wine vinegar
- Salt
- ½ teaspoon soy sauce
- 1 tablespoon toasted sesame seeds

Nutrition Facts (per Serving)

Calories 386 | Fat 3.3 g | Carb 78.4 g

Protein 16.2 g

Fiber 9.2 g

Instructions

1. Add ¼ cup water in your electric pressure cooker and keep a steamer basket inside.
2. Place the sweet potato, parsnip, and carrot in the basket.
3. Secure the lid and turn the pressure knob to SEALING.
4. Press MANUAL (or "PRESSURE COOK" in newer models) and set the timer to 2 MINUTES on HIGH PRESSURE.
5. When the timer beeps, press CANCEL and turn the pressure knob to VENTING and remove the pressure.
6. Open the lid and transfer the cooked vegetables to a bowl. Set aside.
7. Remove the steamer and discard any water.
8. Next, add the black rice and 1¾ cup water to the cooker.
9. Secure the lid and turn the pressure knob to SEALING.
10. Press MANUAL and set the timer to 15 minutes on HIGH PRESSURE.
11. In the meantime, combine shallot + cilantro + lime zest + lime juice + wine vinegar + soy sauce + salt in a mixing bowl. Set aside.
12. When the timer beeps, press CANCEL and allow the pressure to release naturally for 8-10 minutes. Then turn the pressure knob to VENTING and release the remaining pressure.
13. Open the lid and transfer the rice to a serving bowl(s).
14. Add the cooked veggies on top and pour in the dressing. Stir well, garnish with sesame seeds and serve.

Kheer

Sweet and hearty rice porridge.

Preparation Time: 5 minutes

Pressure Time: 20 minutes

Pressure Level: High

Pressure Vent Release: Natural

Servings: 4

Ingredients

- ½ cup basmati rice, soaked for 1 hour
- ½ cup water
- 4 cups coconut milk, full fat
- Pinch of saffron strands
- ½ cup sugar
- ½ teaspoon cardamom powder
- 3 tablespoons chopped cashews
- 3 tablespoons chopped almonds
- 2 tablespoons raisins

Instructions

1. Press SAUTE to heat your electric pressure cooker. Add ½ cup water.
2. Once the water starts to steam, add milk + soaked (and drained) rice. Stir well.
3. Secure the lid and turn the pressure knob to SEALING.
4. Press MANUAL (or "PRESSURE COOK" in newer models) and set the timer to 20 MINUTES on HIGH PRESSURE.
5. When the timer beeps, press CANCEL and allow the pressure to release naturally for 8-10 minutes. Then turn the pressure knob to VENTING and release the remaining pressure.
6. Open the lid and add saffron + sugar + cardamom powder + chopped cashews + almonds + raisins.
7. Press SAUTE and stir continuously until the kheer thickens (takes anywhere from 3-6 minutes, depends on your desired consistency).
8. Press CANCEL, transfer to a serving bowl(s), top it up with more nuts + raisins. Serve hot or chilled.

Nutrition Facts (per Serving)

Calories 683 | Fat 52.2 g | Carb 55.1 g | Protein 16.2 g
Fiber 7.9 g

Baked (but not baked) Beans

No time to bake your beans? Electric Pressure Cooker is your friend! Just remember to soak them up for 6-8 hours.

Preparation Time: 5 minutes

Pressure Time: 15 minutes

Pressure Level: High

Pressure Vent Release: Natural

Servings: 2

Ingredients

- 1 tablespoon olive oil
- ¼ cup finely chopped onion
- 1 cup basic white (navy) beans, soaked for 6-8 hours and drained
- ½ tablespoon dry mustard
- 1 teaspoon smoked paprika
- 1 bay leaf
- 1 cup veggie stock (or water)
- 2 tablespoons chopped dates
- 2 tablespoons tomato paste
- 1 tablespoon blackstrap molasses
- 1 tablespoon Dijon mustard
- ½ tablespoon apple cider vinegar
- Salt, to taste

Instructions

1. Press SAUTE to heat your electric pressure cooker. Add the oil.
2. Once it's hot, add the chopped onion and saute for 2 minutes or until fragrant.
3. Add the beans, mustard, paprika and the bay leaf. Stir well and add the veggie stock.
4. Secure the lid and turn the pressure knob to SEALING. Press MANUAL (or "PRESSURE COOK" on newer models) and set the timer to 15 MINUTES on HIGH PRESSURE.
5. When the timer beeps, press CANCEL and allow the pressure to release naturally for 8-10 minutes. Then turn the pressure knob to VENTING and release the remaining pressure.
6. Remove the lid and test the texture of the beans. If they are not cooked through or aren't soft enough to squish, then cook for 3 more minutes (add water/stock if needed).
7. Discard the bay leaf and add the salt, chopped dates, tomato paste, molasses, Dijon mustard and vinegar. Mix well.
8. Press SAUTE and let it simmer for about 2 minutes. Serve.

Nutrition Facts (per Serving)

Calories 202 | Fat 5.9 g | Carb 36.1 g | Protein 4.7 g

Refried Beans

Preparation Time: 5 minutes

Pressure Time: 20 minutes + 5 minutes

Pressure Level: High + High

Pressure Release: Natural + Quick

Servings: 2

Ingredients

To prepare salsa,

- 1 medium tomato, finely chopped
- 1 medium onion, minced
- 2 garlic cloves, minced
- ¼ teaspoon minced jalapeno

To prepare the beans,

- 1 tablespoon olive oil
- 1 medium onion, diced
- 2 garlic cloves, minced
- 1 teaspoon ground cumin
- ¼ teaspoon chili powder
- ½ teaspoon dried oregano
- ¾ cup black beans, soaked for 10-12 hours
- 1 ¼ cup water
- 1-piece (1-inch) seaweed, preferably kombu
- Dash of salt
- 2 tablespoons freshly chopped cilantro

Instructions

1. To prepare the salsa, combine all the salsa ingredients together in a mixing bowl - onion, tomato, garlic, and jalapeno. Set aside.
2. Press SAUTE to heat your electric pressure cooker. Add oil. Once it's hot, add the diced onion and saute for about a minute. Add the garlic, ground cumin, chili powder and oregano. Cook for another minute, stirring occasionally.
3. Mix in the black beans, water, seaweed and salt.
4. Secure the lid and turn the pressure knob to SEALING.
5. Press MANUAL (or "PRESSURE COOK" on newer models) and set the timer to 20 MINUTES on HIGH PRESSURE.
6. Allow the pressure to release naturally.
7. Open the lid and discard the kombu using tongs.
8. Add the prepared salsa on top. Without stirring or anything, simply put the lid back on, select MANUAL and set the timer to 5 MINUTES on HIGH PRESSURE.
9. When the timer beeps, press CANCEL, turn the pressure knob to VENTING and release the pressure. Open the lid and blend the beans using an immersion blender (blend according to your liking). Season with salt and garnish with freshly chopped cilantro. Serve hot!

Nutrition Facts (per Serving)

Calories 341 | Fat 4.1 g | Carb 61.4 g | Protein 18.3 g
Fiber 14.5 g

Ethiopian Lentil Stew

This is one of many variations of Ethiopian lentils, and it's so full of flavors.

Preparation Time: 10 minutes

Pressure Time: 15 minutes

Pressure Level: High

Pressure Vent Release: Natural

Servings: 2-3

Ingredients

Berbere Spice Mix,

- 1 teaspoon smoked paprika
- ½ teaspoon cayenne pepper
- ½ teaspoon onion powder
- ½ teaspoon garlic powder
- ½ teaspoon cumin powder
- ½ teaspoon coriander powder
- ¼ teaspoon cardamom powder
- ¼ teaspoon clove powder
- ¼ teaspoon cinnamon powder
- Pinch of nutmeg
- Pinch of allspice

Lentil Stew,

- 1.5 tablespoons olive oil
- ½ cup diced onion
- 1 teaspoon grated ginger
- 4 garlic cloves minced
- ½ cup chopped tomatoes
- Salt
- 1 cup red lentils, washed
- 5-6 small-medium potatoes quartered
- 2 cups water
- Cilantro

Instructions

1. To prepare the Berbere, mix all the spices in a bowl and set aside.
2. Time to cook the lentils. Press SAUTE to heat your electric pressure cooker. Add oil.
3. Once it's hot, add onion and saute for 1-2 minutes or until translucent.
4. Add ginger and garlic. Stir and cook for 2 minutes.
5. Add the tomatoes, berbere spice, and salt. Mix well and cook for 3-4 minutes.
6. Add the lentils, potatoes, and 2 cups of water. Stir well.
7. Secure the lid and turn the pressure knob to SEALING. Press MANUAL (or "PRESSURE COOK" on newer models) and set the timer to 15 MINUTES on HIGH PRESSURE.
8. When the timer beeps, press CANCEL and allow the pressure to release naturally for 8-10 minutes. Then turn the pressure knob to VENTING and manually release the remaining pressure.
9. Open the lid and transfer to a serving bowl(s). Garnish with freshly chopped cilantro and serve with rice.

Nutrition Facts (per Serving)

Calories 324 | Fat 7 g | Carb 54.1 g | Protein 17.8 g
Fiber 9.4 g

Lentil Bolognese

Preparation Time: 5 minutes

Pressure Time: 15 minutes

Pressure Level: High

Pressure Vent Release: Natural

Servings: 3-4

Ingredients
- 1 cup whole red lentils (whole masoor), washed
- 4 medium fire-roasted tomatoes, roughly chopped
- 1 medium onion, diced
- 4 garlic cloves, minced
- 3 medium carrots, diced
- 1 can (6 oz.) tomato paste
- 4 cups of water
- 2 tablespoon Italian seasonings
- Salt and pepper
- ¼ teaspoon red pepper flakes
- 2 tablespoons balsamic vinegar

Instructions

1. Add all the ingredients (except vinegar) to your electric pressure cooker and stir.
2. Secure the lid and turn the pressure knob to SEALING.
3. Press MANUAL (or "PRESSURE COOK" on newer models) and set the timer to 15 MINUTES on HIGH PRESSURE.
4. When the timer beeps, press CANCEL and allow the pressure to release naturally for 8-10 minutes. Then turn the pressure valve to VENTING and release the remaining pressure.
5. Open the lid and add balsamic vinegar. Adjust seasonings and serve over pasta or zoodles.

Nutrition Facts (per Serving)

Calories 316 | Fat 8.4 g | Carb 59 g | Protein 17.1 g Fiber 10.7 g

Broccoli & Chickpea Mix

Preparation Time: 5 minutes

Pressure Time: 12 + 1 minutes

Pressure Level: High+ Low

Pressure Release: Natural + Quick

Servings: 2

Ingredients

To prepare the mix,

- ½ cup chickpeas, soaked for 8-10 hours and drained
- 4 garlic cloves, minced
- 1-inch seaweed (kombu)
- ½ cup veggie stock (or water)
- 2 cups broccoli florets
- 1 medium onion, sliced
- Handful of freshly chopped cilantro

To prepare the dressing,

- 1 tablespoon fresh lemon juice
- 1 tablespoon red wine vinegar
- 2 teaspoons Dijon mustard
- 1 teaspoon minced fresh garlic
- 1 tablespoon extra-virgin olive oil
- ½ teaspoon white miso
- Salt and pepper

Instructions

1. Combine the chickpeas, seaweed, garlic and stock/water in your electric pressure cooker.
2. Secure the lid and turn the pressure knob to SEALING.
3. Press MANUAL (or "PRESSURE COOK" on newer models) and set the timer to 12 MINUTES on HIGH PRESSURE.
4. In the meantime, mix all the dressing ingredients in a bowl and set aside.
5. When the timer beeps, press CANCEL and allow the pressure to release naturally for 8-10 minutes. Then turn the pressure knob to VENTING and release the remaining pressure.
6. Open the lid and add the broccoli. Secure the lid, seal the knob, press MANUAL and set the timer to 1 minute on LOW PRESSURE.
7. When timer beeps, press CANCEL and do a quick release. Discard the seaweed and transfer everything into a serving bowl.
8. Add the onion + cilantro and pour the dressing on top. Serve.

Nutrition Facts (per Serving)

Calories 259 | Fat 9.5 g | Carb 23.7 g | Protein 7.5 g
Fiber 6.7 g

Mixed Beans Kwati

Preparation Time: 5 minutes

Pressure Time: 45 minutes

Pressure Level: High

Pressure Vent Release: Natural

Servings: 2

Ingredients

- 1 tablespoon olive oil
- 2 medium onions, chopped
- ¼ cup yellow peas (whole), soaked overnight
- ¼ cup black chickpeas (aka brown chickpeas / gram / kala chana), soaked overnight
- ¼ cup black eyed peas, soaked overnight
- ¼ cup kidney beans, soaked overnight
- ¼ cup pinto beans, soaked overnight
- 1.5 tablespoons ginger-garlic paste
- 3 medium tomatoes, chopped
- ½ teaspoon turmeric
- ½ teaspoon cumin powder
- ½ teaspoon coriander powder
- Salt
- 4 cups water
- Freshly chopped cilantro

Instructions

1. Press SAUTE to heat your electric pressure cooker. Add oil. Once it's hot, add chopped onions and saute for 1-2 minutes or until translucent.
2. Drain the beans and add them to the cooker. Stir and cook for 5 minutes.
3. Add ginger-garlic paste, turmeric, cumin powder, coriander powder, tomatoes and salt. Mix well and cook for another 5 minutes.
4. Add water and give it a quick stir.
5. Secure the lid and turn the pressure knob to SEALING.
6. Press MANUAL (or "PRESSURE COOK" on newer models) and set the timer to 45 MINUTES on HIGH PRESSURE.
7. When the timer beeps, press CANCEL and allow the pressure to release naturally for 8-10 minutes. Then turn the pressure valve to VENTING and release the remaining pressure.
8. Open the lid and mash a portion (around ¼) of the beans using a potato masher.
9. Transfer to a serving bowl(s), garnish with freshly chopped cilantro and serve.

Nutrition Facts (per Serving)

Calories 353 | Fat 5.9 g | Carb 42.6 g | Protein 12.7 g
Fiber 15.1 g

Minty Green Lentil

This lentil is delicious and shines with some fresh mint leaves.

Preparation Time: 5 minutes

Pressure Time: 10 minutes

Pressure Level: High

Pressure Vent Release: Natural

Servings: 2

Ingredients

- 1 tablespoon olive oil
- 1 medium onion, chopped
- 1 cup green lentils (green mung), rinsed
- ½ teaspoon cumin powder
- 1 cup veggie stock/water
- 1 medium carrot, chopped
- ¼ cup fresh mint, chopped
- 2 tablespoons freshly chopped cilantro
- ½ teaspoon grated lemon zest
- 1 tablespoon lemon juice
- Salt and pepper

Instructions

1. Press SAUTE to heat your electric pressure cooker. Add oil.
2. Once it's hot, add the chopped onion and saute for a minute.
3. Mix in the green lentils, cumin powder, and stock/water. Stir.
4. Secure the lid and turn the pressure knob to SEALING. Press MANUAL (or "PRESSURE COOK" on newer models) and set the timer to 10 MINUTES on HIGH PRESSURE.
5. When the timer beeps, press CANCEL and allow the pressure to release naturally for 8-10 minutes. Then turn the pressure knob to VENTING and release the remaining pressure.
6. Remove the lid and test for doneness. If the lentils are not cooked well, cook for 1-2 minutes in the same procedure.
7. Mix in all the remaining ingredients and stir well to mix. Serve.

Nutrition Facts (per Serving)

Calories 362 | Fat 5 g | Carb 62.1 g | Protein 20.4 g
Fiber 11.2 g

Spinach Lentil Mix

Magic of red, yellow, and mung dal with spinach!

Preparation Time: 5 minutes

Pressure Time: 10 minutes

Pressure Level: High

Pressure Vent Release: Natural

Servings: 2

Ingredients

- 1 tablespoon olive oil
- 1 medium onion, chopped
- 2 medium carrots, chopped
- 4 garlic cloves, minced
- ½ teaspoon ground cumin
- ¼ teaspoon ground turmeric
- 3 cups water
- 1 cup mixed lentil (red lentil + yellow lentil + yellow mung), rinsed
- 1 bay leaf
- Salt
- 2 cups fresh spinach, roughly chopped

Instructions

1. Press SAUTE to heat your electric pressure cooker. Add oil.
2. Once it's hot, add onions, garlic, carrots and sauté until onions are translucent.
3. Add turmeric + cumin powder. Stir and saute for 30 seconds. Then add lentils, water, bay leaf, and salt. Mix well.
4. Secure the lid and turn the pressure knob to SEALING.
5. Press MANUAL (or "PRESSURE COOK" on newer models) and set the timer to 10 MINUTES on HIGH PRESSURE.
6. When the timer beeps, press CANCEL and allow the pressure to release naturally for 8-10 minutes. Then turn the pressure knob to VENTING and release the remaining pressure.Open the lid, and remove the bay leaf.
7. Add the chopped spinach and stir. Put the lid back on and let the spinach wilt. Serve hot.

Nutrition Facts (per Serving)

Calories 453 | Fat 16.3 g | Carb 61.1 g | Protein 21.6 g
Fiber 12.5 g

Dal Makhani

Creamy and hearty black lentil.

Preparation Time: 10 minutes

Pressure Time: 35 minutes

Pressure Level: High

Pressure Vent Release: Natural

Servings: 3-4

Ingredients

Soaking (soak for 12 hours),
- 2/3 cup whole black lentils (aka urad dal)
- 1/4 cup kidney beans (aka rajma)

Cooking,
- 3 cloves
- 3 cardamoms
- 1 big cardamom (black cardamom)
- 1 bay leaf
- 2 cinnamon sticks
- ½ teaspoon salt
- 3 cups water

Tempering,
- 2 tablespoons oil (or vegan butter)
- 1 onion
- 3 garlic cloves
- 1-inch ginger
- 2 tablespoons water
- 1 cup tomato puree
- 1/2 teaspoon turmeric powder
- 1/2 teaspoon chilli powder
- 1/2 teaspoon coriander powder
- 1/2 teaspoon cumin powder
- 1/4 teaspoon salt

Garnishing,
- Coconut cream
- Cilantro

Instructions

1. Add whole black lentils + kidney beans + water in a large bowl and soak them for 12 hours.
2. Drain the lentils and add them to your electric pressure cooker. Add cloves, cardamoms, big cardamom, cinnamon sticks, bay leaf, salt, and water.
3. Secure the lid and turn the pressure knob to SEALING.
4. Press MANUAL (or "PRESSURE COOK" on newer models) and set the timer to 35 MINUTES on HIGH PRESSURE.
5. When the timer beeps, press CANCEL and allow the pressure to release naturally for 8-10 MINUTES. Then turn the pressure knob to VENTING and manually release the remaining pressure.
6. Open the lid and make sure the kidney beans are super soft and mushy (if not, cook for 5-8 minutes more).
7. Transfer everything to a large bowl and empty the cooker.
8. Time to make the onion-garlic paste. Add onion + garlic + ginger + 2 tablespoons water to a blender and blend to make a paste. Set aside.
9. Next, press SAUTE and heat the cooker. Once it's dry and hot, add oil + onion-garlic paste. Stir and saute for 4-5 minutes.

10. Add tomato puree, turmeric, chilli powder, cumin powder, coriander powder, and salt. Mix well and cook (with the lid off) for 5 minutes or until the mixture thickens.

11. Stir in the cooked lentils, add 1 cup water and bring it to a boil. Add coconut cream + freshly chopped cilantro and give it a quick stir.

12. That's it. Your vegan dal makhani is now ready. Serve it with rice, roti, naan or pilaf.

Nutrition Facts (per Serving)

Calories 304 | Fat 8.5 g | Carb 42.9 g | Protein 15.7 g
Fiber 9.6 g

Vegan Chili

Preparation Time: 10 minutes
Pressure Time: 2 + 5 minutes
Pressure Level: High+ Low
Pressure Release: Quick + Quick
Servings: 4

Ingredients

- 1 tablespoon olive oil
- 2 medium onions, chopped
- 1 large carrot, diced
- 2 celery stalks, chopped
- 2 green bell peppers, chopped
- 1 jalapeno, seeded and chopped
- 4 garlic cloves, minced
- 2 teaspoons cayenne pepper
- 1 teaspoon smoked paprika
- 1 teaspoon cumin powder
- ¼ teaspoon chipotle chili powder
- Salt
- 4 cups cooked kidney beans
- 2 cups water
- 4 medium fire-roasted tomatoes, roughly chopped
- 2 cups frozen corn, thawed
- ½ cup cracked wheat (bulgur)
- Handful of freshly chopped cilantro
- Lime, to garnish

Instructions

1. Press SAUTE to heat your electric pressure cooker. Add olive oil.
2. Once it's hot, add the veggies - onions, carrots, celery, bell peppers, jalapeno, and garlic. Stir and saute for 4-5 minutes.
3. Add the spices - cayenne pepper, smoked paprika, cumin powder, chipotle chili powder and salt. Stir and cook for 1 minute.
4. Add the kidney beans, water and tomatoes. Stir well, scraping off any brown bits from the bottom.
5. Secure the lid and turn the pressure knob to SEALING.
6. Press MANUAL (or "PRESSURE COOK" on newer models) and set the timer to 2 MINUTES on HIGH PRESSURE.
7. When the timer beeps, press CANCEL, turn the pressure knob to VENTING and release the pressure.
8. Open the lid and stir in corn + bulgur.
9. Again, secure the lid and turn the pressure knob to SEALING.
10. Press MANUAL (or "PRESSURE COOK" on newer models) and set the timer to 5 MINUTES on LOW PRESSURE.
11. When the timer beeps, press CANCEL, turn the pressure knob to VENTING and release the pressure.
12. Open the lid and transfer to serving bowl(s).
13. Garnish with freshly chopped cilantro and drizzle lime juice on top. Serve hot.

Nutrition Facts (per Serving)

Calories 446 | Fat 5.7 g | Carb 81.3 g | Protein 23.3 g
Fiber 24.6 g

Sweet & Spicy Carrots

Preparation Time: 4 minutes

Pressure Time: 4 minutes

Pressure Level: High

Pressure Vent Release: Quick

Servings: 2

Ingredients

- 1/2 cup water
- 4 medium carrots, skin peeled and sliced into bite-sized (~1-inch) pieces
- 1 tablespoon vegan butter (or coconut oil)
- 2 tablespoons maple syrup
- ½ teaspoon ground cumin
- ¼ teaspoon cayenne pepper
- Salt and pepper

Instructions

1. Add 1/2 cup water to your electric pressure cooker. Place a steamer rack inside and distribute the carrot slices on the rack.
2. Secure the lid and turn the pressure knob to SEALING.
3. Press MANUAL (or "PRESSURE COOK" on newer models) and set the timer to 4 minutes on HIGH PRESSURE.
4. When the timer beeps, press CANCEL and turn the pressure knob to VENTING.
5. Carefully remove the rack and drain the water from the cooker.
6. Press saute and add vegan butter (or coconut oil). Once it's hot and melted, add the steamed carrots, ground cumin, cayenne pepper, salt, pepper and stir well.
7. Press CANCEL and add the maple syrup. Stir continuously for 1 minute. Let it cool and serve.

Nutrition Facts (per Serving)

Calories 331 | Fat 14.4 g | Carb 50.9 g | Protein 2.5 g
Fiber 7.1 g

Simple Artichokes with Cashew Dips

Preparation Time: 5 minutes

Pressure Time: 10 minutes

Pressure Level: High

Pressure Vent Release: Natural

Servings: 2

Ingredients

For Artichoke,

- 4 small-medium artichokes, trimmed and cleaned
- 4 garlic cloves, thinly sliced
- 1 cup water/veggie stock
- 2 tablespoons freshly chopped thyme

For Dipping,

- 2/3 cup cashews, soaked for 2 hours
- ¼ cup water
- 2 garlic cloves
- 2 tablespoons lemon juice
- ½ teaspoon lemon zest
- ½ teaspoon apple cider vinegar
- Pinch of salt

Instructions

1. Open up the artichokes and insert the garlic slices in-between the leaves.
2. Add the water (or stock) + thyme in your electric pressure cooker and place a steamer rack inside.
3. Place the artichokes on the rack (make sure the stem side faces up).
4. Secure the lid and turn the pressure knob to SEALING.
5. Press MANUAL (or "PRESSURE COOK" on newer models) and set the timer to 10 MINUTES on HIGH PRESSURE.
6. Meanwhile, combine all the dipping ingredients and blend in a blender until super smooth. Transfer to a bowl and set aside.
7. When the timer beeps, press CANCEL and allow the pressure to release naturally for 8-10 minutes. Then turn the pressure knob to VENTING and release the remaining pressure.
8. Remove the lid and check if the artichokes are well-cooked. If not cook for 2 more minutes (following the same procedure). Dip and serve.

Nutrition Facts (per Serving)

Calories 278 | Fat 11.5 g | Carb 39.1 g | Protein 13.7 g
Fiber 15.2 g

Cauliflower Rice

Easy, gluten-free and delicious cauliflower rice within a couple of minutes.

Preparation Time: 5 minutes

Pressure Time: 1 minutes

Pressure Level: High

Pressure Vent Release: Quick

Servings: 2

Ingredients

- 1 head cauliflower (900 gm. / 2 lb.), washed, leaves trimmed
- ½ cup water
- 1 tablespoon olive oil
- ¼ teaspoon cumin
- ¼ teaspoon coriander
- ¼ teaspoon turmeric
- ¼ teaspoon smoked paprika
- Salt
- Handful of freshly chopped green onion
- 1-2 teaspoons lime juice

Instructions

1. Cut the cauliflower into large chunks and place them in a steamer basket.
2. Transfer the basket to your electric pressure cooker and add 1/2 cup of water.
3. Secure the lid and turn the pressure knob to SEALING.
4. Press MANUAL (or "PRESSURE COOK" on newer models) and set the timer to 1 MINUTE on HIGH PRESSURE.
5. When the timer beeps, press CANCEL, turn the pressure knob to VENTING and release the pressure.
6. Open the lid and transfer the cauliflower to a plate. Remove the water from the cooker.
7. Press SAUTE and allow remaining water to dry. Add oil.
8. Once it's hot, add the cooked cauliflower and break it up using a potato masher. Give it a gentle stir.
9. Add the spices - cumin, coriander, turmeric, paprika and salt. Stir and cook for 3-4 minutes.
10. Transfer to a serving bowl(s). Garnish with a handful of freshly chopped green onions and drizzle lime juice on top.

Nutrition Facts (per Serving)

Calories 229 | Fat 15.3 g | Carb 21.7 g | Protein 8.3 g

Fiber 8.7 g

Asparagus Mushrooms

Preparation Time: 4 minutes

Pressure Time: 2 + 2 minutes

Pressure Level: High + Low

Pressure Release: Quick + Quick

Servings: 2

Ingredients

- 2 teaspoons olive oil
- 1 cup crimini mushrooms, sliced
- 2 garlic cloves, minced
- ¼ cup veggie stock
- 6 oz. (170 gm.) asparagus, bottoms discarded, cut into bite sized pieces
- 5 oz. (140 gm.) sugar snap peas, fiber removed, cut in halves
- 1 tablespoon lemon juice
- 1 teaspoon lemon zest
- Salt and pepper

Instructions

1. Press SAUTE to heat your electric pressure cooker. Add oil.
2. Once it's hot, add the mushrooms and saute for 2 minutes.
3. Add the minced garlic and cook for a minute.
4. Add the veggie stock + salt +pepper and stir well. Secure the lid and turn the pressure knob to SEALING.
5. Press MANUAL (or "PRESSURE COOK" on newer models) and set the timer to 2 minutes on HIGH PRESSURE.
6. When the timer beeps, press CANCEL and turn the pressure knob to VENTING.
7. Remove the lid and add the asparagus. Secure the lid, seal the knob, press MANUAL and set timer to 2 minutes on LOW PRESSURE.
8. Remove the lid and add the sugar snap peas. Put the lid back on and allow to sit for 2 minutes.
9. Sprinkle the lemon juice and zest. Adjust the seasoning and serve.

Nutrition Facts (per Serving)

Calories 323 | Fat 14.9 g | Carb 40.9 g | Protein 10.9 g
Fiber 3.2 g

Easy Garlic Mashed Potatoes

Preparation Time: 3 minutes

Pressure Time: 4 minutes

Pressure Level: High

Pressure Release: Quick

Servings: 2

Ingredients

- 3 large russet potatoes, cut into 1.5-inch chunks
- ½ cup water
- 5 garlic cloves, chopped
- ¼ cup almond milk
- ¼ teaspoon salt
- ¼ teaspoon pepper
- Handful of freshly chopped chives

Instructions

1. Add the potato chunks + water + chopped garlic to your electric pressure cooker.
2. Secure the lid and turn the pressure knob to SEALING.
3. Press MANUAL (or "PRESSURE COOK" on newer models) and set the timer to 4 MINUTES on HIGH PRESSURE.
4. When the timer beeps, press CANCEL, turn the pressure knob to VENTING and release the pressure.
5. Open the lid and transfer everything to a large bowl (discard the liquid, if any), and mash the potatoes with a masher.
6. Gradually add almond milk, salt, and pepper. Once you get the desired consistency, garnish with freshly chopped chives and serve.

Nutrition Facts (per Serving)

Calories 466 | Fat 2.1 g | Carb 103.2 g | Protein 12.5 g
Fiber 7.5 g

Southern Delight

The name says it all, this is a delightful okra recipe!

Preparation Time: 3 minutes

Pressure Time: 2 minutes

Pressure Level: High

Pressure Vent Release: Quick

Servings: 2

Ingredients

- 2 teaspoons olive oil
- 1 large white onion, sliced
- 10 oz. (300 gm.) okra, sliced into 1-inch pieces
- ½ cup corn kernels
- 2 tablespoons water
- 3 medium tomatoes, diced
- 2 tablespoons freshly chopped cilantro
- Salt and pepper, to taste

Instructions

1. Press SAUTE to heat your electric pressure cooker. Add oil.
2. Once it's hot, add the chopped onion and saute for 2 minutes or until fragrant.
3. Add the sliced okra. Stirring continuously, cook for a minute.
4. Stir in the tomatoes, corn, veggie stock, salt, and pepper.
5. Secure the lid and turn the pressure knob to SEALING.
6. Press MANUAL (or "PRESSURE COOK" on newer models) and set the timer to 2 minutes on HIGH PRESSURE.
7. When the timer beeps, press CANCEL and turn the pressure knob to VENTING and release the pressure.
8. Open the lid and transfer everything to a serving bowl. Adjust the seasonings, garnish with freshly chopped cilantro and serve.

Nutrition Facts (per Serving)

Calories 209 | Fat 3.9 g | Carb 32.3 g | Protein 6.2 g
Fiber 6.4 g

Spicy Kale

Preparation Time: 3 minutes

Pressure Time: 5 minutes

Pressure Level: Low

Pressure Release: Quick

Servings: 2

Ingredients

- 1 tablespoon olive oil
- 1 medium onion, diced
- 1 medium bell pepper, diced
- 2 large garlic cloves, minced
- ½ teaspoon ground fenugreek
- 1 teaspoon berbere spice (recipe on Ethiopian Lentil Stew)
- ¼ cup water
- 1 medium bunch marrow-stem kale, de-stemmed and sliced
- Salt and pepper, to taste

Instructions

1. Press SAUTE to heat your electric pressure cooker. Add oil.
2. Once it's hot, add the diced onion and saute for 2 minutes or until fragrant.
3. Add the diced bell pepper, garlic, and all the spices. Stir and cook for about 20 seconds.
4. Scrape the bottom and add water + salt + pepper.
5. Add the kale and give it a quick stir. Secure the lid and turn the pressure knob to SEALING.
6. Press MANUAL (or "PRESSURE COOK" on newer models) and set the timer to 5 minutes on LOW PRESSURE.
7. When the timer beeps, press CANCEL and turn the pressure knob to VENTING and release the pressure.
8. Open the lid, adjust the seasonings and serve warm.

Nutrition Facts (per Serving)

Calories 254 | Fat 15.3 g | Carb 27.4 g | Protein 6.5 g
Fiber 7.5 g

Steamed Garlic Soybeans

Preparation Time: 4 minutes

Pressure Time: 3 minutes

Pressure Level: High

Pressure Release: Quick

Servings: 2

Ingredients

- 1/2 cup water
- 2 cups fresh soybeans / edamame, in their pods
- 1 teaspoon extra virgin olive oil
- 4 large garlic cloves, finely chopped
- 1 tablespoon soy sauce
- Salt and pepper

Instructions

1. Add 1/2 cup water to your electric pressure cooker. Place a trivet + steamer basket inside.
2. Distribute the edamame in the basket.
3. Secure the lid and turn the pressure knob to SEALING.
4. Press MANUAL (or "PRESSURE COOK" on newer models) and set the timer to 3 MINUTES on HIGH PRESSURE.
5. When the timer beeps, press CANCEL and turn the pressure knob to VENTING and release the pressure.
6. Open the lid and transfer the cooked pods to a serving bowl. Remove the trivet and basket from the cooker. Also remove the liquid.
7. Press SAUTE and heat the pressure cooker. Once it's dry and hot, add oil + garlic and saute for 2 minutes or until golden.
8. Press CANCEL and add salt, pepper, soy sauce, and edamame pods. Stir well and serve.

Nutrition Facts (per Serving)

Calories 164 | Fat 8 g | Carb 12 g | Protein 16.1 g
Fiber 5.8 g

Mashed Broccoli

Preparation Time: 3 minutes

Pressure Time: 4 minutes

Pressure Level: High

Pressure Release: Quick

Servings: 2

Ingredients

- 2 large garlic cloves, minced
- 1 tablespoon curry powder
- 4 tablespoons water/veggie stock
- 1 medium head broccoli, sliced
- 1 cup chopped celeriac (or celery root), cut into bite-sized pieces
- 1 cup coconut milk
- 1 tablespoon coconut flakes
- Salt and pepper, to taste

Instructions

1. Press SAUTE to heat your electric pressure cooker.
2. Once it's hot, add the minced garlic, curry powder and dry-saute for 20 seconds.
3. Add the water/veggie stock and stir well. Scrape the bottom, if sticky.
4. Add the broccoli, celery root, coconut milk, coconut flakes, salt and pepper. Give it a gentle stir.
5. Secure the lid and turn the pressure knob to SEALING.
6. Press MANUAL (or "PRESSURE COOK" on newer models) and set the timer to 4 minutes on HIGH PRESSURE.
7. When the timer beeps, press CANCEL, turn the pressure knob to VENTING and release the pressure.
8. Open the lid and blend everything using an immersion blender (or simply transfer the contents to a normal blender) and blend until you get the desired texture. Serve.

Nutrition Facts (per Serving)

Calories 263 | Fat 17.7 g | Carb 23.9 g | Protein 9.3 g
Fiber 10.3 g

Zucchini Herb Summer Veggies

Preparation Time: 4 minutes

Pressure Time: 3 minutes

Pressure Level: High

Pressure Release: Quick

Servings: 2

Ingredients

- 1 tablespoon olive oil
- 1 white onion, thinly sliced
- 1 red bell pepper, thinly sliced
- 3 garlic cloves, thinly sliced
- 4 medium zucchini, sliced into ½ inch pieces
- 4 tablespoons dry white wine
- 3 large tomatoes, diced
- 1 bay leaf
- 3 fresh thyme sprigs
- 3 tablespoons freshly chopped basil
- Salt and pepper

Instructions

1. Press SAUTE to heat your electric pressure cooker. Add oil.
2. Once it's hot, add the sliced onion, bell pepper and garlic. Stir and saute for 2 minutes or until onion-garlic turn golden.
3. Add the zucchini slices. Stir and cook for 3 minutes. Then add the wine and stir, scraping the brown bits from the bottom (if any).
4. Add the diced tomatoes, thyme and bay leaf. Adjust the salt and pepper.
5. Secure the lid and turn the pressure knob to SEALING.
6. Press MANUAL (or "PRESSURE COOK" on newer models) and set the timer to 3 MINUTES on HIGH PRESSURE.
7. When the timer beeps, press CANCEL, turn the pressure knob to VENTING and release the pressure.
8. Open the lid. Remove the bay leaf, top up with chopped basil and serve.

Nutrition Facts (per Serving)

Calories 189 | Fat 7.9 g | Carb 22 g | Protein 4.6 g
Fiber 7.3 g

Jeera Aloo

Delicious cumin roasted potatoes.

Preparation Time: 4 minutes

Pressure Time: 3 minutes

Pressure Level: High

Pressure Vent Release: Quick

Servings: 2

Ingredients

- 750 gm. or 1.5 lb. potatoes
- 1/2 cup water
- 1 tablespoon olive oil
- 1 teaspoon cumin seeds
- 1 onion, sliced
- Pinch of asafoetida (hing)
- ¼ teaspoon turmeric
- ½ teaspoon cayenne pepper
- ½ teaspoon coriander powder
- Salt
- 1 teaspoon dried mango powder
- Freshly chopped cilantro

Instructions

1. Wash, skin, and cut the potatoes into medium chunks.
2. Transfer them to your electric pressure cooker. Add 1/2 cup of water. Secure the lid and turn the pressure knob to SEALING. Press MANUAL (or "PRESSURE COOK" on newer models) and set the timer to 3 MINUTES on HIGH PRESSURE.
3. When the timer beeps, press CANCEL, turn the pressure knob to VENTING and release the pressure. Open the lid, transfer the potatoes to a bowl and set aside. Drain the cooker.
4. Press SAUTE. Once the cooker is hot and dry, add oil + cumin seeds. The seeds will start to splutter and will turn light brown.
5. Then add onion + asafoetida. Stir and saute for 2 minutes or until the onions become golden.
6. Add turmeric, cayenne pepper, coriander powder, salt, and dried mango powder. Stir and cook for 1-2 minutes.
7. Add the boiled potatoes and stir + cook for 1 minute.
8. Sprinkle some freshly chopped cilantro.
9. Your Jeera Aloo is ready! Serve over rice, wraps, or by itself.

Nutrition Facts (per Serving)

Calories 319 | Fat 6.9 g | Carb 67.3 g | Protein 5.2 g
Fiber 5.4 g

The Green Bowl

Preparation Time: 2 minutes

Pressure Time: 5 minutes

Pressure Level: Low

Pressure Release: Quick

Servings: 1

Ingredients

- 1 teaspoon olive oil
- 4 garlic cloves, minced
- Pinch of turmeric powder
- 1 medium bunch (~4 cups) greens - kale/collards (thick stems discarded)
- 2 tablespoons water/veggie stock
- 2 tablespoons tahini
- 1 teaspoon tamari
- 1/2 teaspoon balsamic vinegar
- Salt and pepper

Instructions

1. Press SAUTE to heat your electric pressure cooker. Add oil.
2. Once it's hot, add the garlic and turmeric. Stir and saute for 1 minute.
3. Add the greens, and water (add more water if the greens are tough).
4. Secure the lid and turn the pressure knob to SEALING.
5. Press MANUAL (or "PRESSURE COOK" on newer models) and set the timer to 5 minutes on LOW PRESSURE.
6. When the timer beeps, press CANCEL, turn the pressure knob to VENTING and release the pressure.
7. Open the lid, mix in the tahini and give it a good stir.
8. Transfer to a serving bowl, drizzle tamari and vinegar. Season with salt + pepper and serve.

Nutrition Facts (per Serving)

Calories 182 | Fat 13.3 g | Carb 13.8 g | Protein 6 g
Fiber 3.6 g

Instant Broccoli Mushroom Combo

Preparation Time: 5 minutes

Pressure Time: 2 minutes

Pressure Level: High

Pressure Release: Quick

Servings: 2

Ingredients

- 1 tablespoon olive oil
- 1 medium onion, sliced
- 4 garlic cloves, minced
- 1 teaspoon minced ginger
- 1½ cup sliced mushrooms
- 2½ cups broccoli florets
- 2 tablespoons water
- 1 tablespoon tamari
- 1 tablespoon sesame seeds, toasted
- Salt and pepper

Instructions

1. Press SAUTE to heat your electric pressure cooker. Add oil.
2. Once it's hot, add the chopped onion, garlic and ginger. Stir and saute for 1 minute.
3. Next, add the sliced mushrooms and stir + saute for 3-4 minutes. Then add broccoli florets, water, tamari, salt and pepper. Stir well.
4. Secure the lid and turn the pressure knob to SEALING.
5. Press MANUAL (or "PRESSURE COOK" on newer models) and set the timer to 2 MINUTES on HIGH PRESSURE.
6. When the timer beeps, press CANCEL and turn the pressure knob to VENTING to release the pressure.
7. Open the lid and transfer everything to a serving bowl. Adjust the seasonings. Sprinkle toasted sesame seeds on top and serve.

Nutrition Facts (per Serving)

Calories 126 | Fat 5.8 g | Carb 16.8 g | Protein 5.3 g
Fiber 5.2 g

Sesame & Napa Cabbage

Preparation Time: 4 minutes

Pressure Time: 2 minutes

Pressure Level: Low

Pressure Release: Quick

Servings: 2

Ingredients

- 1 teaspoon sesame oil
- 2 teaspoons sesame seeds
- 1/4 cup water
- 1 medium head napa cabbage leaves
- Salt and pepper
- 2 teaspoons soy sauce

Instructions

1. Add 1/4 cup water to your electric pressure cooker and place a steamer basket inside. Place and stack the napa leaves on the basket.
2. Secure the lid, turn the pressure knob to SEALING, select MANUAL (or "PRESSURE COOK" on newer models) and set the timer to 2 MINUTES on LOW PRESSURE.
3. When the timer beeps, turn the pressure knob to VENTING and release the pressure.
4. Open the lid and transfer the steamed leaves to a large mixing bowl. Add the ingredients - soy sauce, sesame oil, sesame seeds, salt, and pepper. Mix well and serve.

Nutrition Facts (per Serving)

Calories 230 | Fat 5.5 g | Carb 44.2 g | Protein 9.4 g
Fiber 12.5 g

Rosemary Potatoes

Preparation Time: 4 minutes

Pressure Time: 3 minutes

Pressure Level: High

Pressure Release: Quick

Servings: 2

Ingredients

- 1½ tablespoons olive oil
- 1 pound (16 oz. / 450 gm) small fingerling potatoes, pierced twice with a knife
- ¼ cup water
- 1 tablespoon rosemary, freshly minced
- Salt and pepper

Instructions

1. Select SAUTE to heat your electric pressure cooker. Add oil. Once it's hot, add the potatoes and stir. Cook for 5 minutes, stirring regularly.
2. Add ¼ cup water. Secure the lid and turn the pressure knob to SEALING. Select MANUAL (or "PRESSURE COOK" on newer models) and set the timer to 3 MINUTES on HIGH PRESSURE.
3. When the timer beeps, press CANCEL, turn the pressure knob to VENTING and release the pressure.
4. Open the lid and transfer everything to a serving bowl (remove liquid, if any). Season with salt and pepper. Top up with freshly minced rosemary and serve.

Nutrition Facts (per Serving)

Calories 252 | Fat 11 g | Carb 36.3 g | Protein 3.9 g
Fiber 6.1 g

Aloo Gobhi

A must try pressure cooker recipe!

Preparation Time: 4 minutes

Pressure Time: 2 + 1 minutes

Pressure Level: High

Pressure Vent Release: Quick

Servings: 2

Ingredients

- 1 tablespoon olive oil
- 1 teaspoon cumin seeds
- 4 garlic cloves, chopped
- 1/2 tablespoon minced ginger
- 1 medium onion, sliced
- 2 medium potatoes, cut into 2-inch pieces
- 1/2 teaspoon turmeric powder
- 1/2 teaspoon cayenne pepper
- 1/2 teaspoon coriander powder
- 1/2 teaspoon cumin powder
- 1/2 teaspoon garam masala powder
- Salt
- 2 tablespoons water
- 1 medium tomato, chopped
- 1 cup green peas (fresh or frozen)
- 1 medium head cauliflower, cut into large florets
- Handful of freshly chopped cilantro

Instructions

1. Select SAUTE to heat your electric pressure cooker. Add oil.
2. Once it's hot, add cumin. As it starts to splutter, add garlic + ginger + onion. Stir and sauté until the onions turn golden.
3. Add the potato chunks and stir well (around 1 minute).
4. Next add the spices - turmeric, cumin, coriander, cayenne pepper, and salt.
5. Throw in the chopped tomatoes and mix well (around 2 minutes). Then add 2 tablespoons of water and stir.
6. Secure the lid and turn the pressure knob to SEALING.
7. Select MANUAL (or "PRESSURE COOK" on newer models) and set the timer to 2 MINUTES on HIGH PRESSURE.
8. When the timer beeps, press CANCEL, turn the pressure knob to VENTING and release the pressure.
9. Open the lid and add the green peas + cauliflower florets. Mix well to coat.
10. Again, secure the lid, turn pressure knob to SEALING, select MANUAL, and set timer to 1 MINUTE on HIGH PRESSURE. When timer beeps, do a quick pressure release.
11. Garnish with freshly chopped cilantro and serve.

Nutrition Facts (per Serving)

Calories 280 | Fat 8.1 g | Carb 46.9 g | Protein 8.4 g
Fiber 10.2 g

Easy Tomato Soup

Preparation Time: 10 minutes

Pressure Time: 10 minutes

Pressure Level: High

Pressure Vent Release: Natural

Servings: 2

Ingredients

- 1 tablespoon olive oil
- 2 medium onions, chopped
- 2 medium carrots, skin peeled and chopped
- ¼ cup chopped beetroots
- 3 large garlic cloves, finely chopped
- 2 cups of chopped ripe tomatoes
- 1 teaspoon sugar
- 1 cup veggie stock (or water)
- Salt and pepper
- ½ cup tofu puree

Instructions

1. Press SAUTE to heat your electric pressure cooker. Add oil.
2. Once it's hot, add carrots + beetroots + onions and saute for 2-3 minutes or until onions become tender. Stir in the garlic and saute for another minute.
3. Add chopped tomatoes and veggie stock (or water). Give it a quick stir. Secure the lid and turn the pressure knob to SEALING.
4. Press MANUAL (or "PRESSURE COOK" on newer models) and set the timer to 10 MINUTES on HIGH PRESSURE. Once the timer beeps, press CANCEL and allow the pressure to release naturally for 8-10 minutes.
5. Open the lid, add the tofu puree and blend the mixture (using immersion blender if you have one) to get a creamy soup.
6. Add additional stock (or water) to achieve your desired consistency. Sprinkle salt + pepper + sugar and stir. Select SAUTE and simmer for 3-4 minutes. Serve hot.

Nutrition Facts (per Serving)

Calories 301 | Fat 17.7 g | Carb 32.2 g | Protein 8.9 g
Fiber 6.1 g

French Onion Cream Soup

Preparation Time: 4 minutes

Pressure Time: 10 minutes

Pressure Level: High

Pressure Release: Quick

Servings: 2

Ingredients

- 1 tablespoon olive oil
- 3 medium yellow onions, chopped finely
- Salt and pepper
- 1 teaspoon sugar
- ¾ cup dry white wine
- 2 cups veggie stock
- 3 fresh thyme sprigs
- One French bread loaf, cut into 1-inch slices, lightly toasted
- ½ cup vegan cheese, shredded
- 2 tablespoons chopped basil leaves

Instructions

1. Press SAUTE to heat your electric pressure cooker. Add oil.
2. Once it's hot, add onions and saute for 2-3 minutes or until translucent.
3. Add salt, pepper and sugar. Stir and saute for 15 seconds.
4. Pour in the wine. Stir and scrape the brown bits (if any) from the bottom. Cook until most of the wine is evaporated.
5. Next, add the stock + thyme and give it a quick stir.
6. Secure the lid and turn the pressure knob to SEALING.
7. Press MANUAL (or "PRESSURE COOK" on newer models) and set the timer to 10 MINUTES on HIGH PRESSURE.
8. When the timer beeps, press CANCEL, turn the pressure knob to VENTING and release the pressure. Set your oven on Broil.
9. Open the lid and transfer to serving bowls with toasted bread slices. Then evenly sprinkle the shredded cheese on top.
10. Place the bowls in the oven for 3-5 minutes. Garnish with chopped basil and serve hot.

Nutrition Facts (per Serving)

Calories 445 | Fat 19.6 g | Carb 50.4 g | Protein 14.3 g
Fiber 5.7 g

Butternut Squash & Sage Soup

Preparation Time: 10 minutes

Pressure Time: 10 minutes

Pressure Level: High

Pressure Release: Natural

Servings: 2

Ingredients

- 1 tablespoon olive oil
- 6 fresh sage leaves
- 1 medium yellow onion, chopped
- 1 large celery stalk, chopped
- 4 medium garlic cloves, finely chopped
- 2 cups butternut squash - deseeded, skin removed and diced into small cubes
- 3 cups veggie stock (or water)
- ¼ teaspoon baking soda
- Salt and pepper
- ¾ cup tofu puree (blended tofu)
- ¼ teaspoon nutmeg

Instructions

1. Press SAUTE to heat your electric pressure cooker. Add oil.
2. Once it's hot, add sage leaves and saute until crispy. Then transfer the leaves to a paper towel.
3. Add onions and sauté until translucent. Then add garlic + celery and stir well for 2-3 minutes or until fragrant.
4. Add squash, baking soda, veggie stock (or water), salt and pepper. Stir well.
5. Secure the lid and turn the pressure knob to SEALING.
6. Press MANUAL (or "PRESSURE COOK" on newer models) and set the timer to 10 MINUTES on HIGH PRESSURE.
7. When the timer beeps, press CANCEL and allow the pressure to release naturally for 8-10 minutes. Then turn the pressure knob to VENTING and release the remaining pressure.
8. Open the lid and add tofu puree + nutmeg. Using an immersion blender blend everything until smooth.
9. Adjust consistency by gradually adding stock (or water). Press SAUTE and simmer for 4-5 minutes. Transfer to a serving bowl(s), garnish with crispy sage and serve.

Nutrition Facts (per Serving)

Calories 236 | Fat 12 g | Carb 27.5 g | Protein 10.3 g
Fiber 5.3 g

Chickpea Spinach Stew

Preparation Time: 10 minutes

Pressure Time: 20 minutes

Pressure Level: High

Pressure Vent Release: Natural

Servings: 2

Ingredients

- 1 tablespoon olive oil
- 1 medium onion, chopped
- 1 bay leaf
- 4 garlic cloves, chopped
- 1 medium carrot, chopped
- 5 tomatoes, chopped
- ¾ cup chickpeas, soaked overnight
- ½ teaspoon turmeric
- ½ teaspoon coriander powder
- ½ teaspoon cumin powder
- ½ teaspoon cayenne pepper
- Salt
- 3 cups water
- 2 cups spinach, roughly chopped

Instructions

1. Select SAUTE to heat your electric pressure cooker. Add oil.
2. Once it's hot, add onion + bay leaf + garlic. Stir and saute for 2 minutes or until the onions turn golden brown.
3. Add tomatoes and spices. Stir and cook for 2 minutes.
4. Next add the carrots and chickpeas (drained). Stir and cook for another 2 minutes. Add water.
5. Secure the lid and turn the pressure knob to SEALING.
6. Press MANUAL (or "PRESSURE COOK" on newer models) and set the timer to 20 MINUTES on HIGH PRESSURE.
7. When the timer beeps, press CANCEL and allow the pressure to release naturally for 8-10 minutes. Then turn the pressure knob to VENTING and manually release the remaining pressure.
8. Open the lid. Using a potato masher, mash around ¼ portion of the chickpeas.
9. Add the chopped spinach and give it a quick stir.
10. Put the lid back on. The spinach will wilt from the residual heat. Serve hot.

Nutrition Facts (per Serving)

Calories 376 | Fat 8 g | Carb 28.8 g | Protein 16.1 g
Fiber 6.1 g

Kale & Sweet Potato Soup

Preparation Time: 5 minutes

Pressure Time: 10 minutes

Pressure Level: High

Pressure Release: Natural

Servings: 2

Ingredients

- 1 tablespoon olive oil
- 2 medium onions, chopped
- 4 garlic cloves, minced
- 2 large white potatoes or sweet potatoes - skin peeled, washed and cut into bite size cubes
- 4 cups veggie stock (or water)
- Salt and pepper
- 1 cup kale, washed, drained, stemmed and chopped

Instructions

1. Press SAUTE to heat your electric pressure cooker. Add oil.
2. Once it's hot, add onions and garlic. Stir and saute until onions turn translucent.
3. Add potatoes, stock (or water), salt, and pepper. Stir well.
4. Secure the lid and turn the pressure knob to SEALING.
5. Press MANUAL (or "PRESSURE COOK" on newer models) and set the timer to 10 MINUTES on HIGH PRESSURE.
6. When the timer beeps, press CANCEL and allow the pressure to release naturally for 8-10 MINUTES. Then turn the pressure knob to VENTING and release the remaining pressure.
7. Open the lid and mash the potatoes using a masher. Then using an immersion blender, blend everything until creamy. Adjust consistency by gradually adding stock (or water).
8. Throw in the kale, press SAUTE and simmer for 4-5 minutes. Serve hot.

Nutrition Facts (per Serving)

Calories 351 | Fat 14.4 g | Carb 53.6 g | Protein 5.5 g
Fiber 8.7 g

Barley Mushroom Hearty Soup

Preparation Time: 5 minutes

Pressure Time: 15 minutes

Pressure Level: High

Pressure Release: Natural

Servings: 2-3

Ingredients

- 1 tablespoon olive oil
- 1 large onion, chopped
- 8 oz./ 230 gm. mushrooms, coarsely chopped
- ¾ cup dry red wine
- 2 small carrots, skin peeled and chopped
- 2 small celery stalks, finely chopped
- 4 garlic cloves, finely chopped
- 2 thyme sprigs
- 1 bay leaf
- 2 cups veggie stock
- 1 cup water
- ½ cup pearl barley, rinsed
- Salt and pepper

Instructions

1. Press SAUTE to heat your electric pressure cooker. Add oil.
2. Once it's hot, add onions + garlic and sauté for 2 minutes or until fragrant.
3. Add the mushrooms. Stir and saute for 1 minute.
4. Pour wine. Scrape the bottom to collect the bits (if any).
5. Next, add celery, carrots, thyme, bay leaf, water, stock, barley, salt and pepper. Stir well. Secure the lid and turn the pressure knob to SEALING.
6. Press MANUAL (or "PRESSURE COOK" on newer models) and set the timer to 15 MINUTES on HIGH PRESSURE.
7. When the timer beeps, press CANCEL and let the pressure release naturally for 8-10 minutes. Then turn the pressure knob to VENTING and release the remaining pressure. Serve hot.

Nutrition Facts (per Serving)

Calories 363 | Fat 10 g | Carb 61.7 g | Protein 7.3 g
Fiber 8.5 g

Kidney Beans Stew

Preparation Time: 5 minutes

Pressure Time: 30 minutes

Pressure Level: High

Pressure Vent Release: Natural

Servings: 2

Ingredients

- 1 tablespoon olive oil
- 1 onion, chopped
- 2 large garlic cloves, mashed
- 2 small carrots, skin peeled, chopped into small chunks
- 2 large tomatoes, diced
- 1 cup kidney beans, soaked overnight
- 2 cups water
- ½ teaspoon red pepper flakes
- Salt and pepper
- 3 tablespoons parsley leaves, chopped finely

Instructions

1. Press SAUTE to heat your electric pressure cooker. Add oil.
2. Once it's hot, add onion + garlic and saute for 1 minute. Then add carrots, tomatoes, kidney beans, water, red pepper flakes, salt and pepper. Mix well.
3. Secure the lid and turn the pressure valve to SEALING.
4. Press MANUAL (or "PRESSURE COOK" on newer models) and set the timer to 30 MINUTES on HIGH PRESSURE.
5. When the timer beeps, press CANCEL and let the pressure release naturally for 8-10 minutes. Then turn the pressure knob to VENTING and release the remaining pressure.
6. Open the lid, stir in parsley. Adjust seasonings and serve.

Nutrition Facts (per Serving)

Calories 429 | Fat 16.4 g | Carb 61 g | Protein 14.5 g
Fiber 14.5 g

Split Peas Soup

Preparation Time: 5 minutes

Pressure Time: 20 minutes

Pressure Level: High

Pressure Release: Natural

Servings: 2-4

Ingredients

- 5 cups water
- 1 large sweet potato, peeled and diced
- 1 cup green split peas
- ½ cup navy beans, rinsed
- 1 bay leaf
- ½ teaspoon smoked paprika
- Salt and pepper
- 4 tablespoons nutritional yeast

Instructions

1. Add all the ingredients (except nutritional yeast) to your electric pressure cooker and stir.
2. Secure the lid and turn the pressure knob to SEALING.
3. Press MANUAL (or "PRESSURE COOK" on newer models) and set the timer to 20 MINUTES on HIGH PRESSURE.
4. When the timer beeps, press CANCEL and allow the pressure to release naturally for 8-10 minutes. Then turn the pressure knob to VENTING and release the remaining pressure.
5. Open the lid and add nutritional yeast. Mix well, adjust seasonings and serve hot.

Nutrition Facts (per Serving)

Calories 459 | Fat 6.1 g | Carb 83.4 g | Protein 30.3 g

Fiber 29 g

Black Bean Soup

Preparation Time: 5 minutes

Pressure Time: 20 minutes

Pressure Level: High

Pressure Release: Natural

Servings: 2

Ingredients

- 1 tablespoon olive oil
- 1 large onion, diced
- 1 cup black beans, soaked overnight
- ½ teaspoon cumin powder
- ½ teaspoon chipotle chili powder
- Salt and pepper
- 3 cups water
- 2 cups frozen corn kernels, thawed
- 1 cup salsa
- Handful of freshly chopped cilantro

Instructions

1. Press SAUTE to heat your electric pressure cooker. Add olive oil.
2. Once it's hot, add diced onion and saute until it turns golden.
3. Add the black beans and spices - cumin, chipotle chili powder, salt, pepper. Stir and cook for 2 minutes.
4. Next add water and give it a quick stir.
5. Secure the lid and turn the pressure knob to SEALING.
6. Press MANUAL (or "PRESSURE COOK" on newer models) and set the timer to 20 MINUTES on HIGH PRESSURE.
7. When the timer beeps, press CANCEL and allow the pressure to release naturally for 8-10 minutes. Then turn the pressure knob to VENTING and release the remaining pressure.
8. Open the lid and check for doneness.
9. For a creamier texture, you can blend it using an immersion blender (or a normal blender). Add the corn + salsa.
10. Press SAUTE and simmer for 3-4 minutes. Garnish with freshly chopped cilantro and serve hot.

Nutrition Facts (per Serving)

Calories 524 | Fat 7 g | Carb 92.7 g | Protein 28.3 g
Fiber 21.2 g

Creamy Minty Pea Soup

Preparation Time: 2 minutes

Pressure Time: 5 minutes

Pressure Level: High

Pressure Vent Release: Quick

Servings: 2

Ingredients

- 2 teaspoons olive oil
- 1 bay leaf
- 1 cinnamon stick (small)
- 4 garlic cloves, chopped
- 1 onion, sliced
- 2 cups green peas (fresh or frozen)
- 1 cup water
- 1 cup fresh mint leaves
- Salt and Pepper
- ¼ cup coconut cream

Instructions

1. Select SAUTE to heat your electric pressure cooker. Add oil.
2. Once it's hot, add bay leaf, cinnamon stick, garlic, and onion.
3. Stir and saute for 2 minutes or until the onions turn golden.
4. Add the green peas and mix well. Then add 1 cup of water.
5. Secure the lid and turn the pressure knob to SEALING.
6. Press MANUAL (or "PRESSURE COOK" on newer models) and set the timer to 5 MINUTES on HIGH PRESSURE.
7. When the timer beeps, press CANCEL, turn the pressure knob to VENTING and release the pressure.
8. Open the lid, press SAUTE and add the mint leaves. Stir and cook for 1 minute. Press CANCEL.
9. Remove and discard the bay leaf and cinnamon stick.
10. Using an immersion blender (or a normal blender), blend the mixture until creamy. Add water to adjust the consistency (if desired).
11. Add salt, pepper and coconut cream. Mix well and combine. Reheat if necessary. Serve hot.

Nutrition Facts (per Serving)

Calories 324 | Fat 7.7 g | Carb 59.6 g | Protein 8.6 g
Fiber 9.4 g

23486974R10042

Made in the USA
Middletown, DE
15 December 2018